THE VICTORY IN CHRIST

COMIC BOOK SERIES

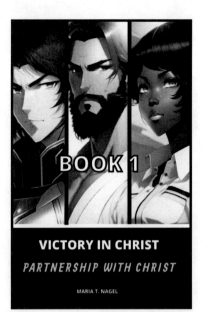

BOOK 1

VICTORY IN CHRIST

PARTNERSHIP WITH CHRIST

MARIA T. NAGEL

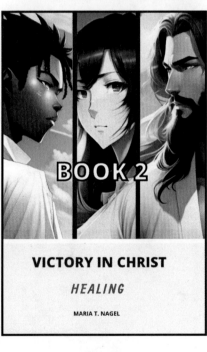

BOOK 2

VICTORY IN CHRIST

HEALING

MARIA T. NAGEL

BOOK 3

VICTORY IN CHRIST

SPIRITUAL WARFARE

MARIA T. NAGEL

THE AFRICA & DIASPORA EDITION

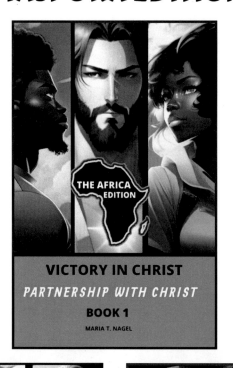

THE AFRICA EDITION

VICTORY IN CHRIST

PARTNERSHIP WITH CHRIST

BOOK 1

MARIA T. NAGEL

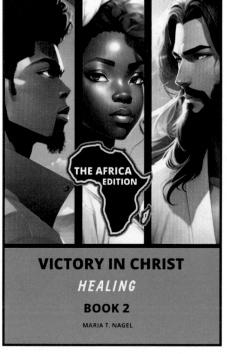

THE AFRICA EDITION

VICTORY IN CHRIST

HEALING

BOOK 2

MARIA T. NAGEL

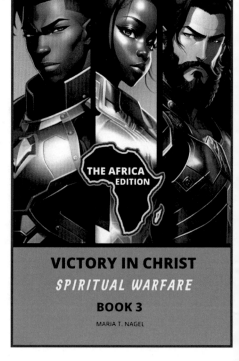

THE AFRICA EDITION

VICTORY IN CHRIST

SPIRITUAL WARFARE

BOOK 3

MARIA T. NAGEL

FOR WOMEN & TEEN GIRLS

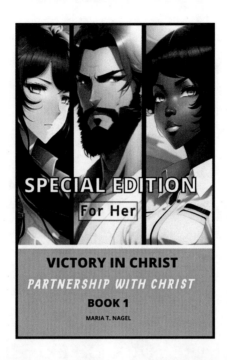

SPECIAL EDITION
For Her

VICTORY IN CHRIST
PARTNERSHIP WITH CHRIST
BOOK 1
MARIA T. NAGEL

SPECIAL EDITION
For Her

VICTORY IN CHRIST
HEALING
BOOK 2
MARIA T. NAGEL

SPECIAL EDITION
For Her

VICTORY IN CHRIST
SPIRITUAL WARFARE
BOOK 3
MARIA T. NAGEL

SCAN ME

**SCAN THIS QR CODE
FOR DIRECT ACCESS
TO THE AMAZON REVIEW PAGE**

SHARE YOUR EXPERIENCE

Digital Artwork by NexSphere
Concept, text, design and creation
by Maria T. Nagel

Christian Spiritual Warfare

*is the act of combating evil influences
through fasting and prayers based
on bible verses.*

*Jesus offers hope, strength, guidance and
protection to those who call upon Him
in the midst of daily struggles
and spiritual battles.*

He comes to steal, kill and destroy.

John 10:10

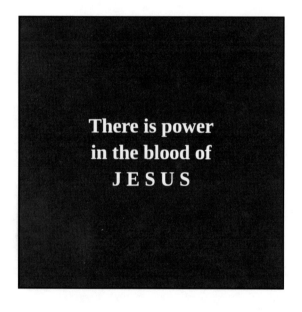

There is power
in the blood of
J E S U S

Having disarmed principalities
and powers, He made a public
spectacle of them, triumphing
over them in it. Colossians 2:15

Be still, and know
that I am God.
Psalm 46:10

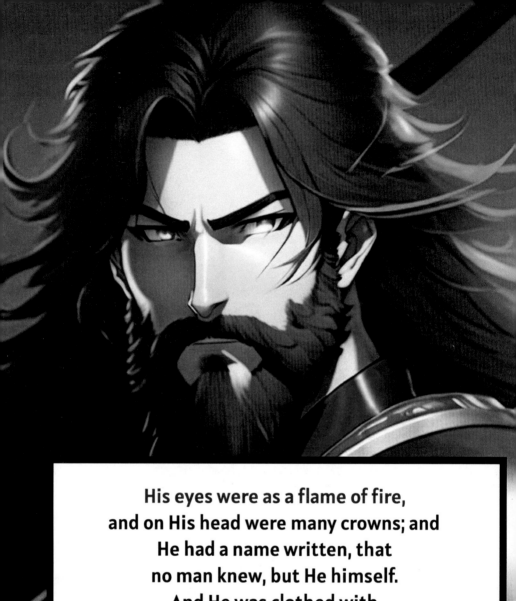

His eyes were as a flame of fire,
and on His head were many crowns; and
He had a name written, that
no man knew, but He himself.
And He was clothed with
a vesture dipped in blood:
and His name is called The Word of God.
Revelation 19:12-13

5

The word of God is alive and powerful.
It is sharper than the sharpest two-edged
sword, cutting between soul and spirit,
between joint and marrow.
It exposes our innermost thoughts
and desires. Hebrews 4:12

Every plant not planted
by my heavenly Father will be uprooted.
Matthew 15:13

She is clothed with strength and dignity, and she laughs without fear of the future Proverbs 31:25

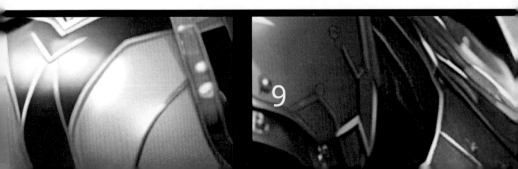

No weapon turned against you will succeed.
You will silence every voice raised up
to accuse you. These benefits are enjoyed
by the servants of the LORD;
their vindication will come from me.
I, the LORD, have spoken! Isaiah 54:17

And it shall come to pass in that day,
that his burden shall be taken away
from off thy shoulder, and his yoke
from off thy neck,
and the yoke shall be destroyed because
of the anointing. Isaiah 10:27

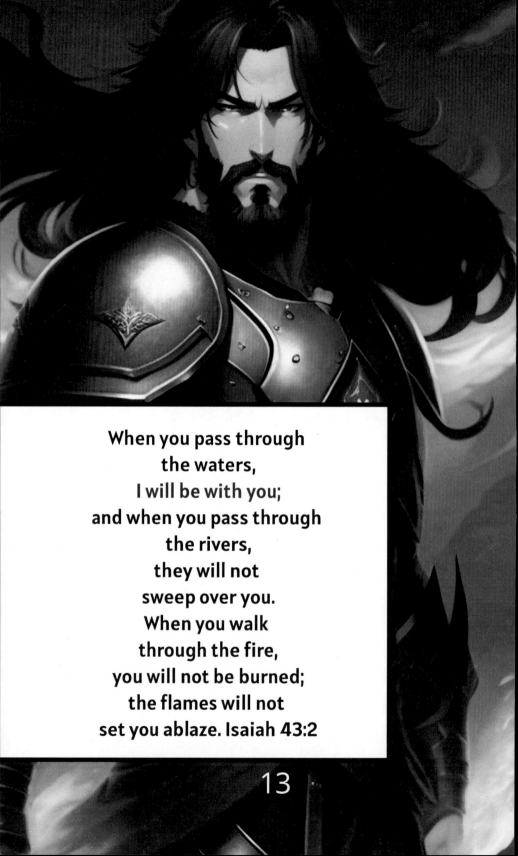

When you pass through
the waters,
I will be with you;
and when you pass through
the rivers,
they will not
sweep over you.
When you walk
through the fire,
you will not be burned;
the flames will not
set you ablaze. Isaiah 43:2

13

11 Put on the full armor of God, so that you can take your stand against the devil's schemes. 12 For our struggle is not against flesh and blood, but against the rulers, against the authorities, against the powers of this dark world and against the spiritual forces of evil in the heavenly realms. 13 Therefore put on the full armor of God, so that when the day of evil comes, you may be able to stand your ground, and after you have done everything, to stand. 14 Stand firm then, with the belt of truth buckled around your waist, with the breastplate of righteousness in place, 15 and with your feet fitted with the readiness that comes from the gospel of peace. 16 In addition to all this, take up the shield of faith, with which you can extinguish all the flaming arrows of the evil one. 17 Take the helmet of salvation and the sword of the Spirit, which is the word of God.
Ephesians 6:11 – 17

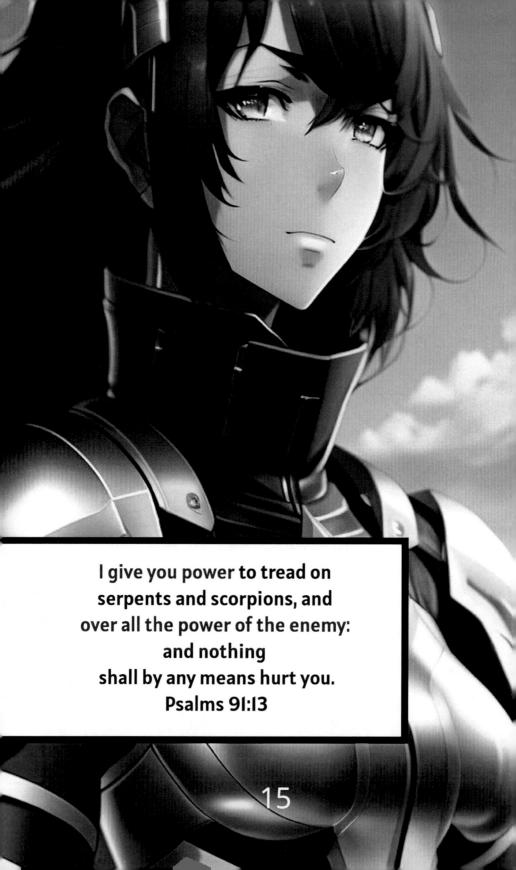

I give you power to tread on
serpents and scorpions, and
over all the power of the enemy:
and nothing
shall by any means hurt you.
Psalms 91:13

15

Believe.

16

Many are the afflictions
of The righteous:
but the LORD delivereth
him out of them all.
Psalms 34:19

Then they cried unto the LORD
in their trouble, and he delivered them
out of their distresses. Psalms 107:6

18

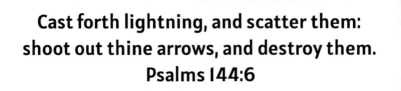

Cast forth lightning, and scatter them:
shoot out thine arrows, and destroy them.
Psalms 144:6

19

20

Do not touch My anointed ones,
And do My prophets no harm.
Psalm 105:15

21

22

He will not allow your foot
to be moved;
He who keeps you
will not slumber. Psalms 121:3

The LORD will cause your enemies who rise
against you to be defeated before you.
They shall come out against you one way
and flee before you seven ways.
Deuteronomy 28:7

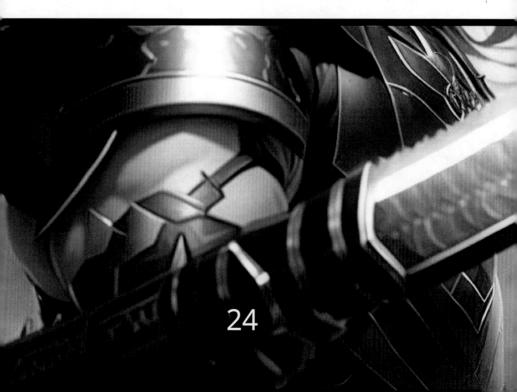

The name of the LORD is a strong tower:
the righteous runneth into it, and is safe.
Proverbs 18:10

26

Behold, the LORD'S hand
is not shortened, that it cannot save;
neither his ear heavy that it cannot hear.
Isaiah 59:1

27

For God has not given us a spirit of fear
and timidity, but of power, love,
and self-discipline. 2 Timothy 1:7

28

If God is for us, who can be against us?
Romans 8:31

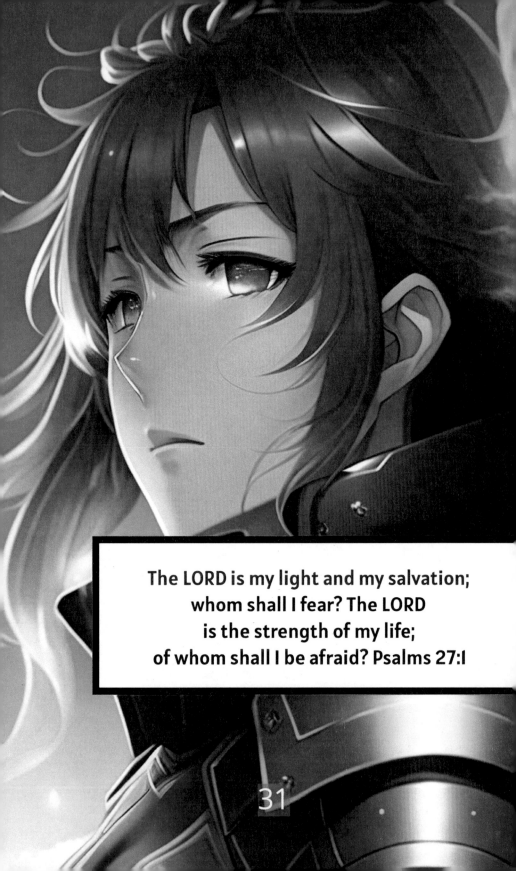

The LORD is my light and my salvation;
whom shall I fear? The LORD
is the strength of my life;
of whom shall I be afraid? Psalms 27:1

31

You are my hiding place and
my shield; I put my hope
in Your word.
Psalms 119:114

32

The LORD is my rock,
and my fortress, and
my deliverer; my God,
my strength, in whom
I will trust; my buckler,
and the horn of my salvation,
and my high tower. Psalms 18:2

33

The Lord is my helper, and I will not fear
what man shall do unto me.
Hebrews 13:6

34

It is God who avenges me,
And subdues the peoples under me;
He delivers me from my enemies.
You also lift me up above those who rise
against me; You have delivered me
from the violent man.
2 Samuel 22:48-49

Victorious through Jesus!

I am not afraid of ten thousand enemies
who surround me on every side.
Arise, O LORD! Rescue me, my God!
Slap all my enemies in the face!
Shatter the teeth of the wicked!
Salvation belongs to the LORD.
Your blessing is upon Your people.
Psalms 3:6-8

Rescue me from my enemies, LORD;
I run to you to hide me. Psalms 143:9

But you, O LORD, are a shield around me;
you are my glory,
the one who holds my head high.
Psalms 3:3

39

He lifted me out of the slimy pit,
out of the mud and mire;
he set my feet on a rock and gave me
a firm place to stand. Psalms 40:2

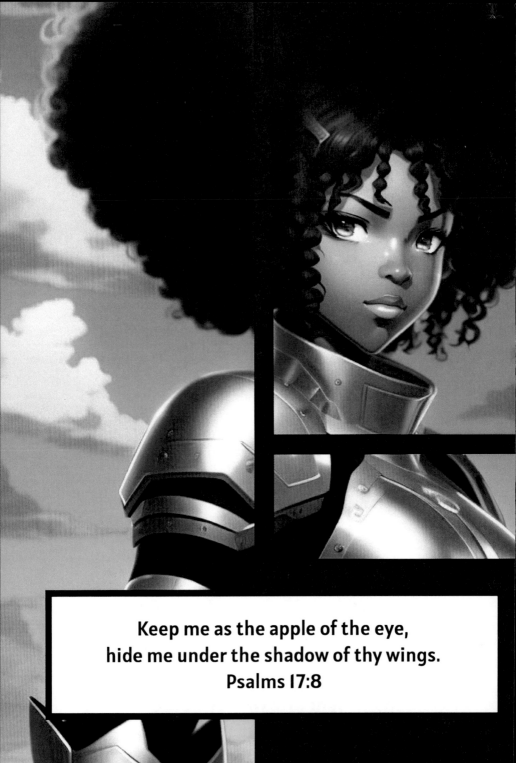

Keep me as the apple of the eye,
hide me under the shadow of thy wings.
Psalms 17:8

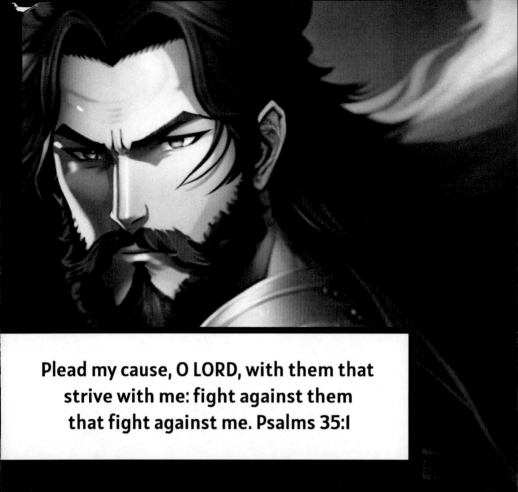

Plead my cause, O LORD, with them that strive with me: fight against them that fight against me. Psalms 35:1

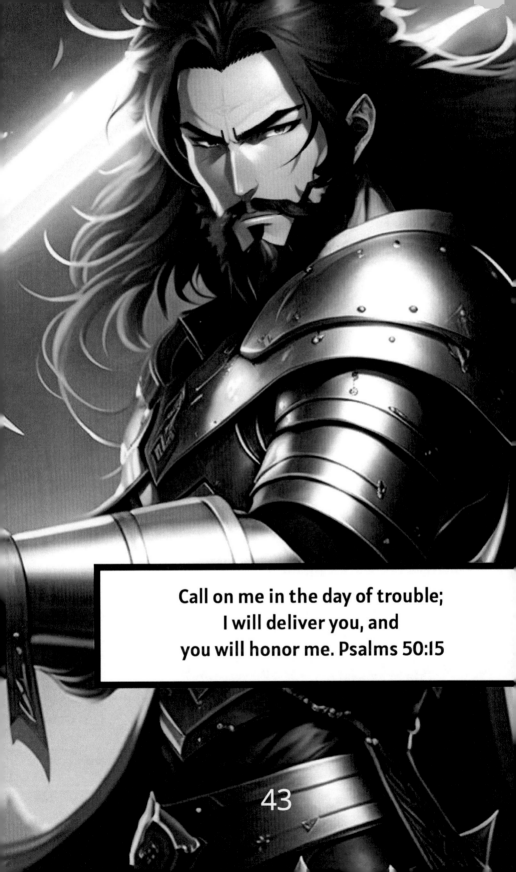

Call on me in the day of trouble;
I will deliver you, and
you will honor me. Psalms 50:15

43

Made in United States
North Haven, CT
07 November 2023